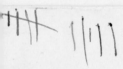

BIRDS
ARE FLYING

This Is a Let's-Read-and-Find-Out Science Book

BIRDS ARE FLYING

Written and illustrated by

John Kaufmann

Thomas Y. Crowell   New York

Other *Let's-Read-and-Find-Out Science Books* You Will Enjoy

Bats in the Dark by John Kaufmann · *Birds at Night* by Roma Gans · *Birds Eat and Eat and Eat* by Roma Gans · *Bird Talk* by Roma Gans · *Ducks Don't Get Wet* by Augusta Goldin · *Emperor Penguins* by Kazue Mizumura · *Hummingbirds in the Garden* by Roma Gans · *It's Nesting Time* by Roma Gans · *Little Dinosaurs and Early Birds* by John Kaufmann · *Streamlined* by John Kaufmann

Let's-Read-and-Find-Out Science Books are edited by Dr. Roma Gans, Professor Emeritus of Childhood Education, Teachers College, Columbia University, and Dr. Franklyn M. Branley, Astronomer Emeritus and former Chairman of The American Museum-Hayden Planetarium. For a complete catalog of *Let's-Read-and-Find-Out Science Books,* write to Thomas Y. Crowell, Department 363, 10 East 53rd Street, New York, New York 10022.

For Herb Johnson

Birds are flying in the park and at the beach. They are flying in fields, in the woods, and over the sea. Birds are flying almost everywhere.

Some birds are flying fast.

CHIMNEY SWIFT

Others are flying slowly.

GREAT BLUE HERON

Some are standing still in the air.

KESTREL

And some are even going backward!

RUBY-THROATED HUMMINGBIRD

3

Why are birds such good fliers? Is it because they
have wings and feathers? It can't be that, because
all birds have wings and feathers, but not all birds
can fly.

Ostriches and penguins can't fly. They are too heavy. Their wings are too small. Their wing muscles are too weak for flying.

RED-TAILED HAWK

But most birds can fly. One important reason is because they are light. Birds are much lighter than other animals their size. This hawk is about the size of a cat. But the cat weighs three times more than the hawk.

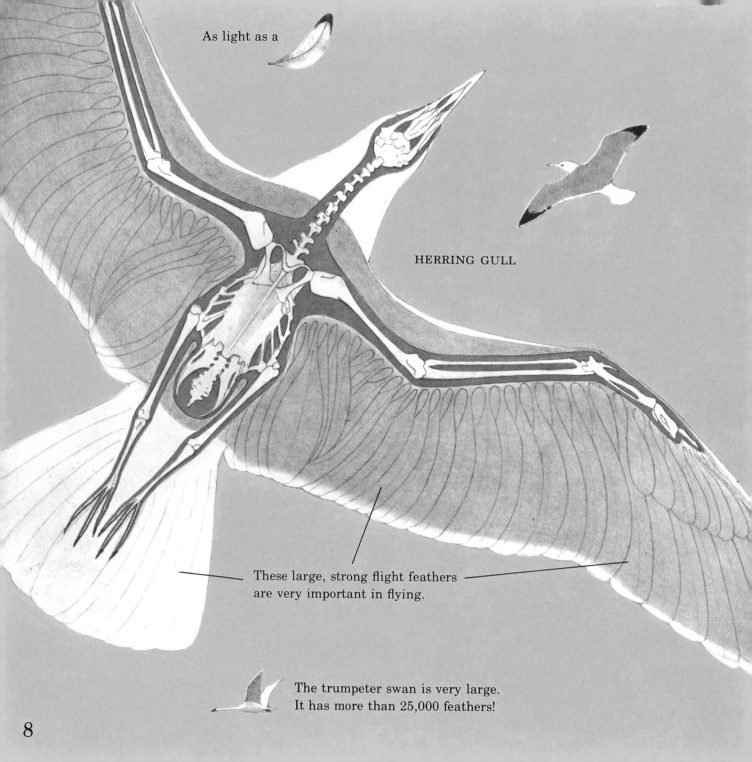

As light as a

HERRING GULL

These large, strong flight feathers
are very important in flying.

The trumpeter swan is very large.
It has more than 25,000 feathers!

8

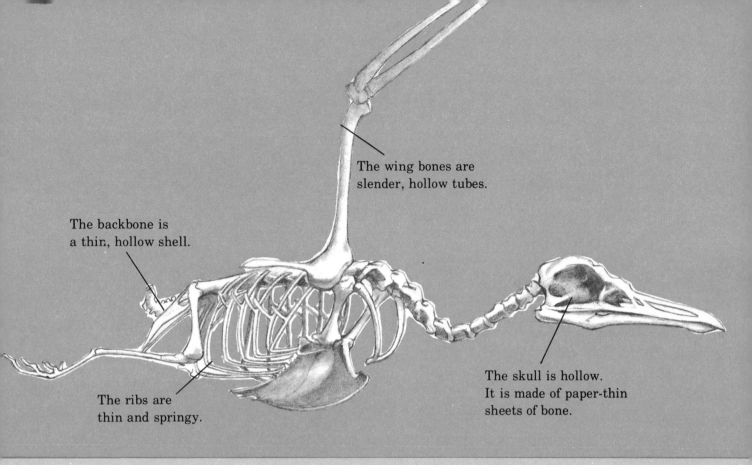

The wing bones are
slender, hollow tubes.

The backbone is
a thin, hollow shell.

The skull is hollow.
It is made of paper-thin
sheets of bone.

The ribs are
thin and springy.

Birds are light because they are mostly feathers,
and feathers do not weigh very much at all.

The skeletons of birds are also light. Birds do not
have as many bones as most other animals. Their
bones are thin. A lot of their bones are hollow.

BLUEBIRD

BLACK-CAPPED CHICKADEE

Birds are light, but they are strong. When birds fly, air pushes hard against them. The big feathers in their wings and their tails bend, but they do not break.

Some of the bones bend, too. The bones in the wings are long and thin, but they are very strong. Like the big feathers, they bend, but they do not break.

BROAD-WINGED HAWK

11

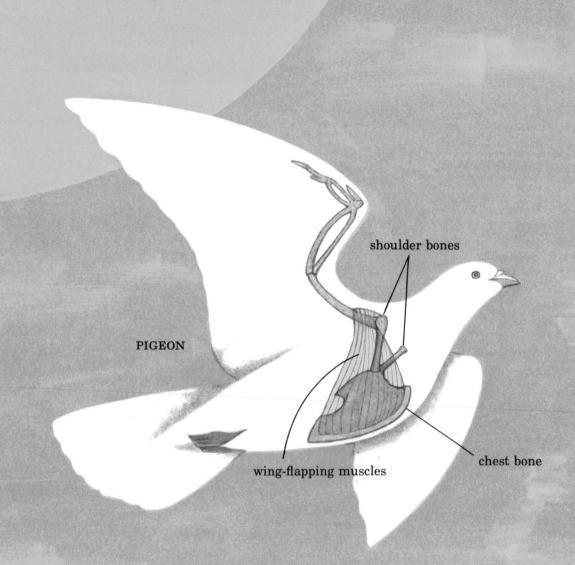

shoulder bones

PIGEON

wing-flapping muscles

chest bone

12

Other bones do not bend. A bird's chest bone is very stiff, and so are the shoulder bones. The muscles that move the wings are fastened to these bones.

Birds have big, powerful wing muscles. Birds use these muscles to flap their wings up and down, up and down, up and down. The flapping wings move the bird through the air.

BLACK-CAPPED CHICKADEE

Swifts flap their wings and fly very fast. They move through the air at more than 97 kilometers (60 miles) an hour. Sometimes they fly even faster. One person measured the speed of swifts at 322 kilometers (200 miles) per hour. That is much faster than the fastest running animal, the cheetah. Its top speed is only 113 kilometers (70 miles) per hour.

CHIMNEY SWIFT

15

Swifts can fly fast, and they can fly all day long. Sometimes they even fly at night. They snap up flying insects as they go. They hardly ever stop to rest. Swifts are the fastest of all birds in flapping flight.

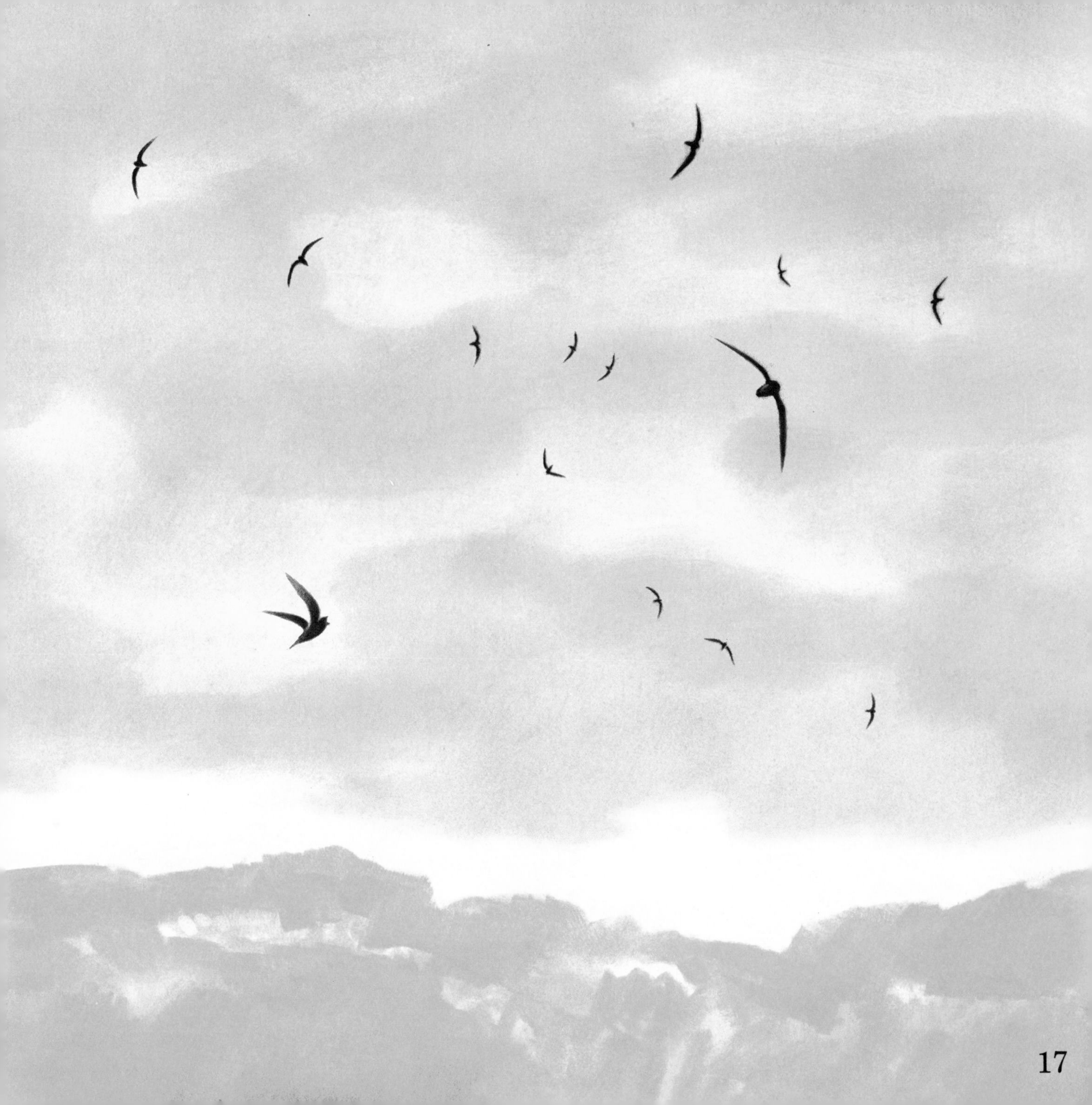

Crows are slow fliers. They usually fly
about 40 kilometers (25 miles) an hour. As
they flap along, they look for food on the ground.
By flying slowly, they can search carefully.

But crows do not always fly slowly. When they
are in danger, they flap harder and faster. They
quickly pick up speed to get away.

The hummingbird can fly fast, but it can also fly very, very slowly. It can even stay in one place in midair. When it feeds, sipping nectar from a flower, it hovers in the air like a helicopter. To hover, it flaps its wings back and forth as fast as eighty times a second.

RUBY-THROATED HUMMINGBIRD

The hummingbird can even go backward. When it finishes sipping, it tilts its wings, backs up, and darts away to another flower.

PEREGRINE FALCON

Some birds can fly without flapping their wings. The falcon often flies this way. The falcon eats other birds. It flies high in the sky, watching for a bird in the air below. When it sees a bird, the falcon folds its wings and drops steeply, head first toward the ground. It dives after the bird. Whoosh! The falcon can dive at 322 kilometers (200 miles) an hour.

23

The vulture can also fly without flapping its wings. But instead of folding its wings and diving, it spreads its wings and holds them still. It is gliding.

The vulture's big wide wings hold it up. It is a large bird, but it does not weigh very much. It can stay up so easily that it seems to float through the air. As the vulture glides, it searches for dead animals on the ground.

TURKEY VULTURE

Sometimes a vulture seems to go straight up. It is riding on a current of warm air that is rising. As the air moves upward, it carries the vulture with it. The vulture is soaring. Higher and higher the big bird goes until it is just a speck in the sky.

TURKEY VULTURE

Many birds fly in more ways than one.
Pigeons flap,

but they also glide.

Sea gulls soar,

but they also flap,

and they can dive to make a quick landing.

All birds must flap hard to take off.

Birds go fast or slow.

They soar up and dive down.

They glide along.

Some birds stay in one place in midair,
and they even go backward.

Go out and watch them. You'll see for yourself the different ways that birds fly.

About the Author

As a child, John Kaufmann says, he was fascinated with birds and how they flew, and he liked to make and fly paper airplanes. Now, years later, his early interest is reflected in the carefully researched, knowledgeable books he writes and illustrates.

A native New Yorker, Mr. Kaufmann was graduated from the Aeronautical Course at Brooklyn Technical High School. He studied art at the Pennsylvania Academy in Philadelphia and during a year's stay in Europe with his wife Alicia. The Kaufmanns and their sons, Darius and Noel, live in Fresh Meadows, New York, where many birds flit through the trees and fly high in the sky.